Under the Mango Tree

Vivean V Pomell

First published in 2023
© 2023, Vivean V Pomell, United Kingdom
Under the Mango Tree, Vivean V Pomell

ISBN print: 9781739336912
ISBN e-book: 9781739336936

All rights reserved. No part of this book may be reproduced, scanned, stored in a retrieval system, or distributed in any form including printed or electronic without prior written permission from the author. Please do not participate in or encourage piracy of copyrighted materials.

Edited by: Vivean V Pomell
Cover design by: Vivean V Pomell
Proofread by: LOGOS West Midlands CIC (Gilbert R Pomell)
Typeset by: LOGOS West Midlands CIC (Gilbert R Pomell)
Illustrations by: Vivean V Pomell
All images have been used with permission.

Although the author has made every effort to ensure that the information in this book was correct at the time of publishing, and while this publication is designed to provide accurate information on the subject matter covered, the author assumes no responsibility for errors, inaccuracies, omissions, or any other inconsistencies, and hereby disclaims any liability to any party for any loss, damage, or disruption caused by errors or omissions, whether such errors or omissions result from negligence, accident, or any other cause.

What is the Windrush?

The Ship MV Empire Windrush: The Windrush generation is named after the ship MV Empire Windrush, which brought the first wave of Caribbean immigrants to the UK in 1948.

The Journey: The voyage of the MV Empire Windrush began in Jamaica and made stops in Mexico and several European countries before arriving in England.

First Arrivals: The ship arrived in Tilbury Docks, Essex, on June 22, 1948, with four hundred and ninety-two passengers from the Caribbean.

Post-War Labor Shortage: The arrival of the Windrush generation was partly in response to post-World War II labour shortages in the UK. Many Caribbean immigrants came to help rebuild the country.

Windrush Day: June 22nd is now celebrated as Windrush Day in the UK, commemorating the contributions of the Windrush generation and their descendants to British society.

Diverse Nationalities: The Windrush generation included people from various Caribbean nations, including Jamaica, Trinidad and Tobago, Barbados, and more.

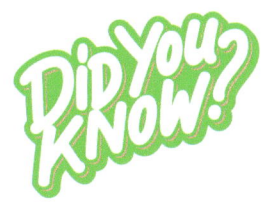

Varied Professions: The Windrush generation worked in a wide range of professions, including healthcare, transport, education, and manufacturing.

Political and Cultural Impact: The Windrush generation significantly influenced British culture, politics, music (notably reggae), and cuisine (such as jerk chicken and roti).

Struggles and Achievements: Despite facing discrimination and challenges, many members of the Windrush generation and their descendants have succeeded in various fields of work.

Citizenship Issues: In recent years, the Windrush scandal highlighted the challenges faced by some members of the Windrush generation who were wrongly classified as illegal immigrants due to documentation issues.

Legacy of Resilience: The Windrush generation's story is one of resilience, determination, and the pursuit of a better life, making it an integral part of Britain's history and multicultural identity.

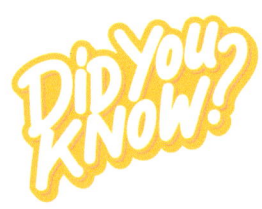

 # Introduction

In the beautiful shade of the mango trees, we gather to celebrate the 75th anniversary of Windrush, where the echoes of the past harmonize with the voices of the future. "Under the Mango Tree" is a mesmerizing collection of poetry that pays homage to the remarkable journey and enduring legacy of the Windrush generation, as witnessed through the eyes and words of the next generation.

Within these pages, a chorus of diverse voices emerges, capturing the spirit of resilience, cultural heritage, and the profound impact that the Windrush generation has had on our lives. As poets, we are both inheritors and torchbearers of their stories, entrusted with the responsibility to honour their legacy and carry their narratives forward and onto the next generations. forward and onto the next generations.

"Under the Mango Tree" invites you to embark on a poetic odyssey that traverses the realms of memory, identity, and belonging. Through vivid imagery and evocative verses, we invite you to immerse yourself in the range of emotions and experiences that shape our connection to the Windrush journey.

In our poems, we explore the intertwined themes of migration, heritage, and the pursuit of dreams. We draw inspiration from our forefathers and foremothers who guide us, acknowledging the sacrifices and courage of those who paved the way for us to flourish in a land that was once unfamiliar. Through the universal language of poetry, we seek to bridge the generational gap, weaving together the threads of our collective history.

As we navigate the landscapes of love, loss, joy, and resilience, we pay tribute to the Windrush generation's indomitable attitude. Their stories are interwoven with our own, forging a profound sense of belonging and a shared responsibility to honour their struggles, triumphs, and contributions.

"Under the Mango Tree" celebrates the vibrancy of our multicultural heritage, the beauty of diversity, and the power of unity. It is an invitation to reflect, to contemplate, and to join in the celebration of our shared journey. Each poem encapsulates a moment, a memory, and an emotion that resonates deep within us.

Through this collection, we pay homage to the past, acknowledge the present, and look into the future. We recognize the strength and resilience of our ancestors while embracing the responsibility to shape a more inclusive and equitable world for generations to come.

Join us as we gather under the mango tree, a symbol of community, wisdom, and ancestral bonds, to celebrate the remarkable 75-year journey of the Windrush generation. Let the poetry within these pages transport you to the heart of their triumphs, struggles, and the enduring legacy they have left us. May these verses resonate in your hearts, spark conversations, and continue the beautiful tapestry of storytelling that the Windrush generation has gifted us.

Why was this book necessary?

I wrote "Under the Mango Tree," a poetry book, as a second-generation child with children of my own to commemorate the 75th anniversary of Windrush for several profound reasons. Firstly, I recognized the immense significance of this historical milestone. The Windrush generation's arrival in the United Kingdom marked a pivotal moment in our shared history, reshaping the cultural fabric of the nation. I felt a deep responsibility to pay homage to their enduring legacy.

As a second-generation child, I wanted to bridge the generational gap and ensure that the stories, struggles, and triumphs of the Windrush pioneers were passed down to my children and future generations. Through poetry, I sought to create a captivating and emotionally resonant narrative that would engage younger audiences and foster a sense of connection to our heritage.

"Under the Mango Tree" became a labour of love, a tribute to the sacrifices made by the Windrush generation, and a celebration of their resilience, determination, and cultural richness. Through the power of poetry, I aimed to capture the essence of their journey, ensuring that their indomitable spirit continues to inspire and educate, 75 years after their historic voyage.

In essence, my poetry book became a testament to the enduring legacy of the Windrush generation, a bridge between generations, and a heartfelt expression of gratitude for the transformative impact they had on the United Kingdom and our lives.

Vivean Viola Pomell

What is Windrush?

The term "Windrush" is historically associated with the MV Empire Windrush, a ship that played a significant role in the mass migration of people from Caribbean countries to the United Kingdom. The Windrush generation refers to the people who arrived in the UK between 1948 and 1971, primarily from Caribbean countries, in response to post-World War II labour shortages and to help rebuild the UK.

The name "Windrush" comes from the ship that brought the first major group of this group of generation to the UK. On June 22, 1948, the MV Empire Windrush arrived at Tilbury Docks in Essex, England, carrying four hundred and ninety-two passengers from the Caribbean, mostly from Jamaica. These individuals and their descendants are collectively referred to as the Windrush generation.

The Windrush generation made significant contributions to various aspects of British society, including healthcare, education, transportation, and culture. They played a crucial role in shaping the multicultural and diverse nature of modern Britain.

In recent years, the term "Windrush" has also been associated with the Windrush scandal, which brought to light the mistreatment and injustices faced by some members of this generation and their descendants, including wrongful deportations and denial of citizenship rights. This led to increased awareness and efforts to rectify these issues and recognize the contributions of the Windrush generation to the UK.

Paying Tribute Through Verse

We, the second and third generations, wrote Windrush's 75th-anniversary poems to honour the pioneers, share their stories, and celebrate their enduring legacy.

Through verse, we bridge generations, ensuring the profound impact of the Windrush lives on. These poems are our tribute to resilience, diversity, and the unity of our heritage.

Come and have a read of our poems!

Crash, bang, woosh
went the uncontrolled
waves.
Hurry, hurry, rush, rush,
rush
trampled the Jamaican
people
onto a large boat called
the Windrush

Aliya, 12

In the land of Windrush,
a tale unfolds,
Of brave souls seeking,
new paths to behold.
They sailed with hope,
their spirits high.
Leaving behind the familiar,
reaching for the sky.

Nia, 11

Amidst the Windrush's gentle breeze,
Legends were born, their spirits at ease.
Their legacy, a sympathy of strength and might,
Forever etched in history's wondrous light.

Rayshaan, 13

My nan always talks about
Being from the tropics
and sitting by the sea,
Exotic fruits like mangoes
and coconuts dangling
From the tree,
But I see none of that,
Each day I am greeted
by English tea.

Jayden, 12

Wind rush wind rush wind rush
A life from lush to mush
The talented swept up
faster than gravity
Just to make England
great again.

Imaan, 11

From the Caribbean shores,
they set sail,
Their journey marked
by a courageous trial.
To the United Kingdom,
they made their way,
Contributing their talents
day by day.

T'kiyah, 16

The Windrush generation,
full of strength and grace,
Carrying dreams and hopes
to a new place.
Their journey, a testament
to resilience and might,
Their stories, a beacon,
shining so bright.
With all their might.

Lasharna, 14

The arrival was under an Act of Law
which made people British citizens
yet they are still questioned
Ancestors need visas
I am mad, I am sad
This is very
very bad

Angelle, 14

Finally, I'm able
to find a new home
In a new country
Making England feel like
sugar and spice
Yes, sugar and spice

Amaya, 11

On a gigantic ship, they came
with a special Windrush name.
Leaving their homes, a long long way,
Trying to find somewhere new to stay.
With excitement and bravery, they set sail.
Facing challenges, without fail.

Amani, 10

I would feel sad,
down in the dumps, distraught.
How would you feel?

Taye, 10

New life
No sun
More work
Less fun
Today I leave
for the UK
Life. Fun. Sun

Shakira, 16

Jamaican vibes fun, joy,
Across the water
To spread our vibrant sounds
Vibrant smells
Jamaican I am.
Jamaican I stand
The boat to the 'promised land'
of opportunity, a place for unity

Marcus, 10

Fine, I FEEL fine
No sun just cold
but I AM FINE
Left my family
but I AM FINE.
If I AM NOT
I will be fine
So fine
yet thick
the feeling
in my throat
when I leave
to make the boat

Ariah, 12

New life
No sun
More work
Less fun
Today I leave
to the UK
Life. Fun. Sun

Shakira, 16

I feel
Sad
Upset
Angry
No sun
No fun

Kamaya, 6

In healthcare, education and more,
The Windrush generation
Opened new doors.
They built communities,
Strong and united,
Their impact on society
Truly ignited.

Sharday, 16

The Windrush generation,
a beacon of light,
Their legacy shines,
forever bright.
In their strength and resilience,
we find inspiration,
A testament to the power
of determination.

Rayhaan, 15

The Windrush. A tale to be told,

Of brave souls seeking a future to unfold.

They sailed on the Empire Windrush's deck,

To a land where dreams and hopes intercept,

Who knows what will happen next.

Kiara, 13

I feel sad and mad
because I had
to leave my home.

Kimiah, 6

Are you British?
You made us come here
But are you British?
What is British?

Akeem, 12

From hot to cold, from Sun to Snow

From happy to sad, from good to bad

Why oh why ask, if they are not valued

Overworked, overrun, overturned.

I'm over it. I want to run. To be free

Pat, 14

They asked us to come,
but are they welcoming
Are we welcoming
They asked us to come,
but we do not belong,
They asked us to come.
Why did they ask?

Nia, 17

Windrush hopes and dreams

Leaving the sunny island of Jamaica's embrace,
I grab my suitcase, a journey to a distant place.
England calls, aboard the Windrush ship I go,
But my suitcase carries no clothes for rain or snow.

In the land of new beginnings, under skies so grey,
I pondered, "What do I do?" on that chilly day.
A job, I knew, was the key to stay warm and bright,
To clothe myself in the face of England's frosty bite.

I'll miss this paradise, the place I call my home,
No more breadfruit, mangoes, or seashores to roam.
No more swims in Dunn's River, its waters crystal-clear,
Yet in this new chapter, I'll find a way to persevere.

For the Windrush carries dreams, and hope resides within,
As I step onto foreign shores, where a new life will begin.
In the face of change and challenge, I'll proudly stand,
With courage in my heart, and a suitcase in my hand.

Vivean

The Windrush, the Windrush, was no real rush.

My people were invited to travel over four and a half thousand miles to make Britain Great.

It was no RUSH for my people who accepted the challenge to be uprooted from our land of Jamaica to plant new roots in a foreign land. A land that was not flowing with milk or honey. Suffice it to say, we boarded HMT Windrush and set sail for England.

Now that we are here, our people were made to suffer because there was no room in the inn, or so, they said. So, up, and down we trod the street until we could find a place to rest our heads. The place we found was small, but we made it home until we could settle from the rush we experienced on HMT Windrush.

The legacy lives on, the physical pain is long gone, but the mental pain lingers on. We will never forget the Windrush because it gave us false hope of better things to come, which proved to be so for England, but left many of us still wishing we had missed the RUSH, that we know call the Wind Rush experience.

Gilbert

Generation Windrush

Is that really your name?
Is that really the title to underline your fame?
Named after the boat,
But what does it mean,
What of the people traversing our seas,
I talk of today,
The people right now,
A child's hands-on school railings,
Another holds tight to a bow,
Looking to the unknown,
They can only reach out,
Wondering what their brave new world is about,
Back to the deck,
Sit at the desk,
Today you will learn,
Tomorrow's the test,
Just try your best,
All to Jesus the rest,
Ask how they felt?,

What were you thinking?
Oh, I was just glad we stayed afloat,
At least we're not sinking,
The minds of the greats,
Just like our own,
But blinded by their horizon,
Cast long shadows over the seeds they'd sown,
Rooted and grounded by those we can't understand,
Happy or not we were held by their hands,
It was hot, but hush,
But don't cry too much,
As they say here,
Needs must,
Keep on keeping on,
Learn wisdom, just trust.

Nathanael

Longing for Home

I long for home to dip my toes in the sea
Those special moments will always be part of me
Back home on that sunny island, Jamaica
Thanking God always who is my maker
Thinking back about those tall mango trees
Swaying in that cool island breeze

Came over for a better life
But was often met with strife
Persevered on because Forward still is Jehovah's will
Despite the bashing and the bad attitudes
I chose to be civil

It's my time to rest
My life surely involved many tests
As I look at my children and grandchildren
My wife and I went through it for a reason
We worked hard for my family's future
But constantly felt under pressure

Through and through
The Lord's been there for me
He has often reminded me
that I must be like a tree
I have proven Him every day
As I aspire to follow His will and way
Trust the Lord and let Him take care of you
And always remember there is value in you

Bethany

In the wake of Windrush, a tale we must share,
Of those who journeyed with hope, bound for a new lair,
They did menial work, tasks others cast aside,
Yet through hardship and toil, their resilience they'd hide.

In a land far from home, they faced racism's cruel sting,
Bearing wounds deep within, memories they'd rarely bring,
For they knew the next generation would walk a brighter way,
They laid the path with sacrifice, come what may.

With dreams in their hearts and courage in their stride,
They sowed seeds of progress, with love as their guide,
Through trials and tribulations, they forged a new day,
So the next generation could have a brighter say.

Now, it's our turn, the torch is passed on,
To seize every opportunity until the darkness is gone,
In the footsteps of Windrush, we must boldly stand tall,
Their legacy of strength, it's our time to install.

With the past as our teacher and their stories our songs,
We'll shatter each barrier, correct every wrong,
For the Windrush generation, with their hope and their grace,
Paved the way for our future, in this challenging space.

So let us remember the struggles they bore,
With each step we take, we honour them more,
With unwavering spirit, we'll reach heights unknown,
For the next generation, a bright future to own.

Viola

The Hope To Come

In the Windrush's wake, a new generation blooms,
The children of courage, with inherited tunes.
Born in a land where dreams intertwine,
The third generation, proud, vibrant, and fine.

From the corners of the Caribbean, they set sail,
Seeking hope and a future that would prevail.
Their journey was arduous, a test of might,
But their spirit soared, like a bird in flight.

Now the torch has been passed to their children, so bold,
The Windrush's legacy, forever to hold.
In the streets of London, their stories unfurl,
The sounds of resilience, vibrant as a whirl.

With a rhythm in their bones and songs in their heart,
They channel the struggles, the pain, and the art.
Their voices rise high, like a soulful refrain,
Revelling in the beauty of cultural terrain.

In their homes, the spices mingle and blend,
Traditions cherished, a heritage to defend.
From reggae to calypso, the beats echo loud,
Delighting the senses with a melodic shroud.

They carry the essence of resilient souls,
Determined to conquer and shatter the moulds.
Their parents' triumphs embedded in their DNA,
The Windrush markers guiding their way.

Through creativity's lens, they rewrite the script,
Painting stories of triumph, never letting it slip.
United, they stand, diverse yet the same,
The third generation, they conquer in name.

So let the world witness this vibrant treasure,
The legacy of Windrush, a boundless pleasure.
For in the third generation, hope intertwines,
A testament to courage, where love always shines.

Louisa

To a cryptic place
Called tilbury dock
They waltzed the street
very very proud
People discriminated against
Them out loud
Fighting through the pain
Many went to the grave
With no gain
And that is my view
On my family's
Windrush pain

Deja

Within the Windrush's gentle flow
Stories of triumph and unity grow
Their journey, a testament of love and pride,
Their legacy, a beacon that we'll never hide.

Mel

In the realm of Windrush's embrace,
Lives intertwined, a tapestry of grace.
Their courage and resilience, a timeless song,
Their legacy echoes forever strong.

Lemar

Challenges they faced,
unfair and unjust,
The Windrush scandal,
a breach of trust.
But their spirit preserves,
undeterred,
Their stories and voices
will not be unheard.

Rechae

Upon the ocean's hushed sigh,
A story is unfolding beneath the skies.
A magnificent journey aboard the Windrush,
Dreams were transported to a distant world.

With billowing waves and salty air,
A woven promise, bold and fair,
They arrived from the Caribbean.
A new name in search of riches

Windrush Minds, a thriving stream
They carved their route within a dream,
to England's shores, a promising beginning,
united destinies, aching hearts.

In bustling cities, they found their place,
Contributing culture, a vibrant space,
Resilient spirits, strength untold,
Their stories in history's pages unfold.

Despite difficulties, they maintained their strength,
A colourful thread in a lengthy tapestry,
Justice fought, voices were shouted,
They lit the trail for equality.

The Windrush legacy: a story to be told
The strength and grace of those who rose up
and battled valiantly will never be separated.
A tale that instilled hope in people's hearts.

Oh, Windrush, a symbol of might and honour,
Your time travels cause our hearts to collide.
A tribute to hopes that survive,
and your legacy is untarnished.

Faith Brynel

What would they do
without my grandparents?
We have survived the world war
We have a vaccination for the flu.
Premature babies can now live
from 24 weeks.
What would they do
without my grandparents?

Deja

Built

Through roads dismantled,
Fallen off course,
Through little remorse;
We built.

Though some in the railways,
Factories were fuller,
And with some on the buses
could they just afford sugar,

Past in and past out.
Jobseekers sought solidity,
To keep what was earned
maintain solidarity.

Through little chance awarded,
Through a restlessness sustained,
By Faith in hope believing,
We changed and made
We built.

Destiny

Swish, swish swoosh, the wind.
They made them rush
now we call it Windrush.
The people who helped,
the people who saved
I argue to be further enslaved.
SWISH, SWISH, SWOOSH,
THE WIND.
Will you rush?

Shanta

Windrush Child

As you board the ship you wonder why
You heard your mother say
you're moving away to a mysterious place
you heard was great
Thirty days later, you arrive in shock
To a cryptic place called Tilbury Dock
They waltzed the street, very very proud
People discriminated against them out loud
Fighting through the pain
Many went to the grave
With no gain and that is my view
On my family's Windrush pain

Deja

Third Generation Poetry Bookmarks

Third Generation Poetry Bookmarks

The third-generation children embarked on a heartfelt project to commemorate the 75th anniversary of Windrush. With creativity and passion, they crafted unique bookmarks, each adorned with their own designs and artwork. Some of these bookmarks were even graced with original poems that beautifully encapsulated the spirit and journey of the Windrush generation.

These young artists poured their hearts and talents into this project, using it as a canvas to express their deep appreciation for the sacrifices and contributions of the first-generation Windrush. The bookmarks became not just tokens of remembrance but also powerful symbols of gratitude and respect.

In a touching gesture, these specially crafted bookmarks were presented to the first generation of Windrush, creating a poignant connection between generations. This act of recognition and celebration bridged the generational gap, allowing the younger members of the community to express their profound respect and admiration for the trailblazing pioneers of the Windrush era.

The bookmarks serve as enduring reminders of the Windrush legacy, a testament to the enduring impact of this remarkable generation on British society. They also symbolize the continuity of the Windrush story, carried forward by the generations that followed, ensuring that the lessons and achievements of the past are never forgotten.

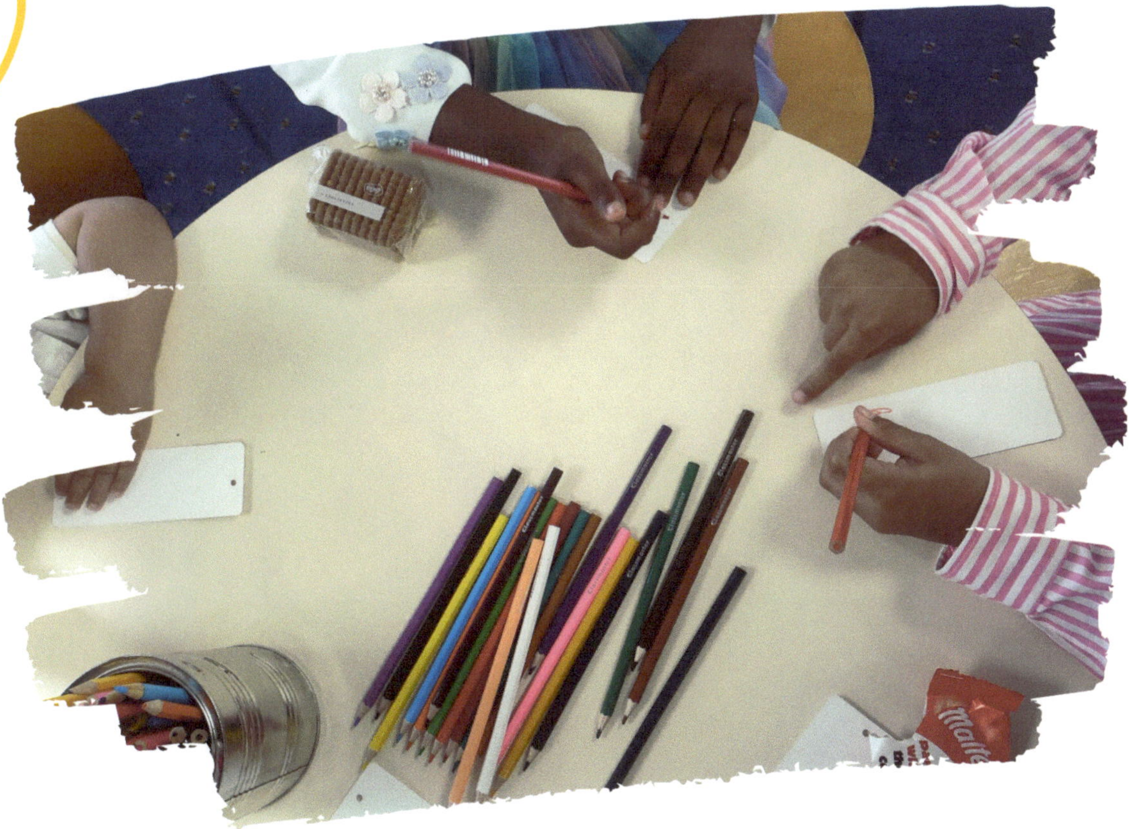

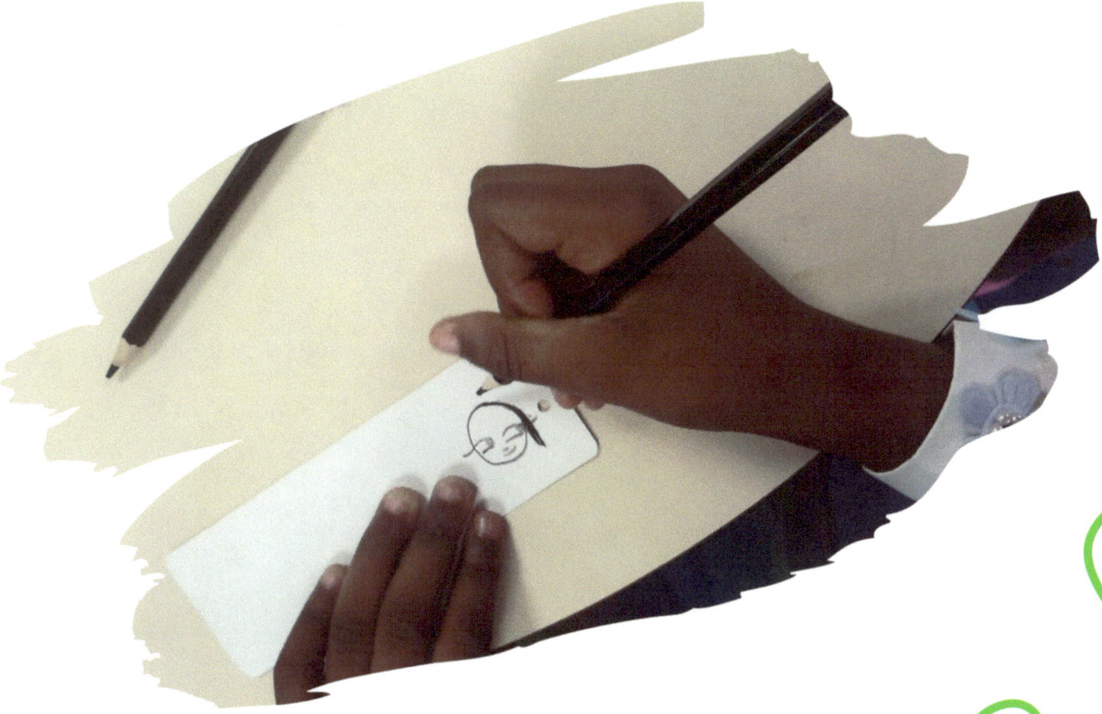

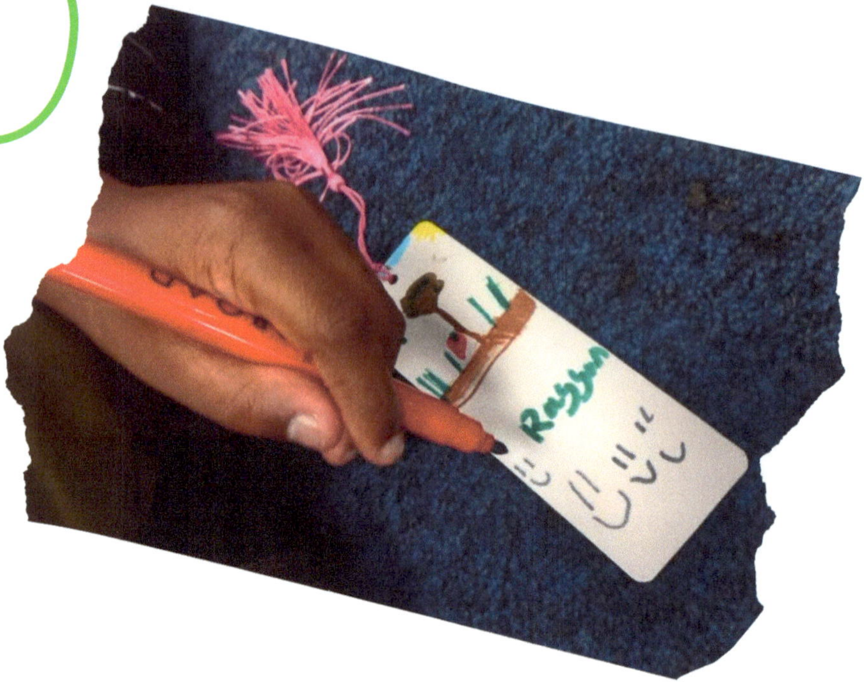

Arrived under IA act as british citizens. Now their ancestors need visas. I am mad, sad, this is bad!
Yes, sugar and spice.
- Angry
- Sad
- Confused
Sad
upset
mad

we call
helped,
people who
wind.
you rush?
I'd feel . . .
sad
distraught
how valued
you feel

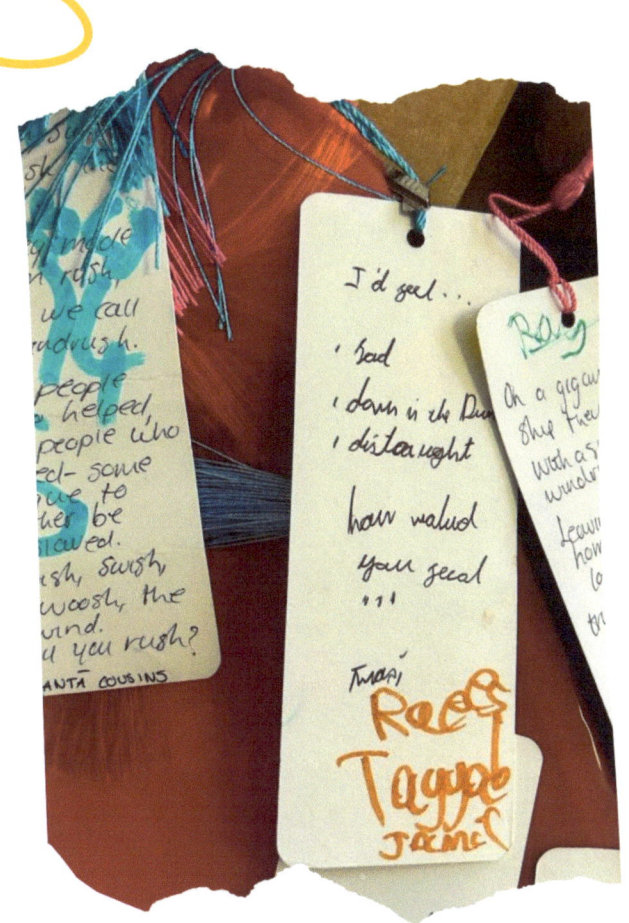

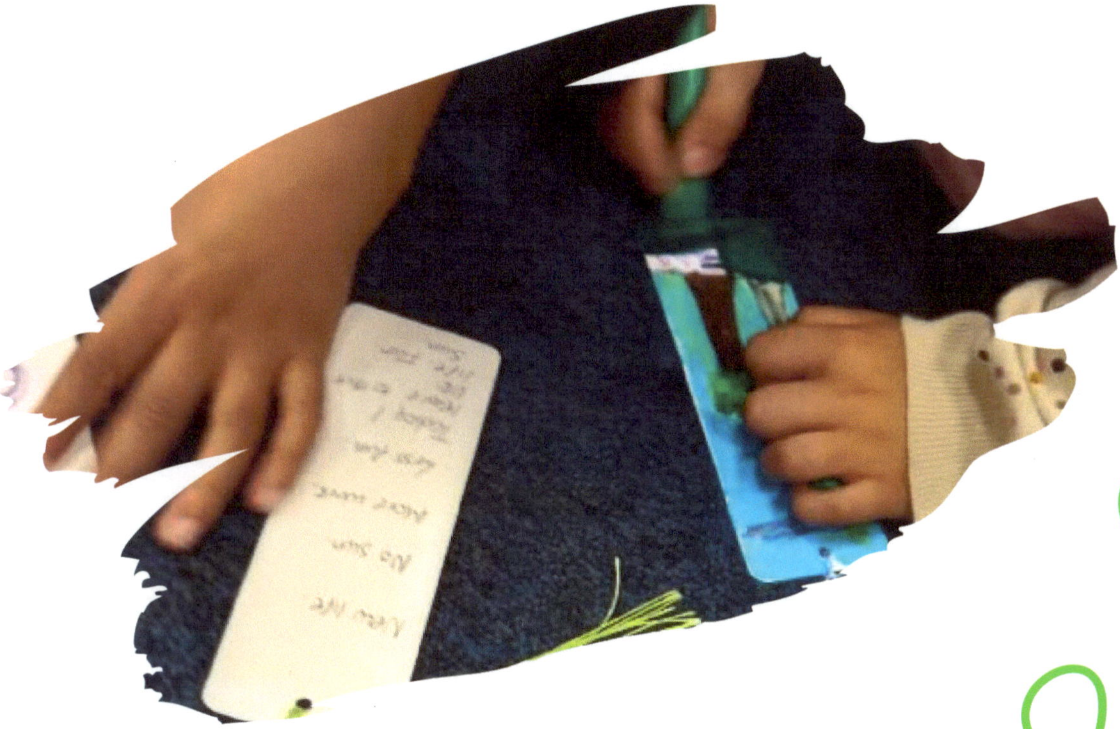

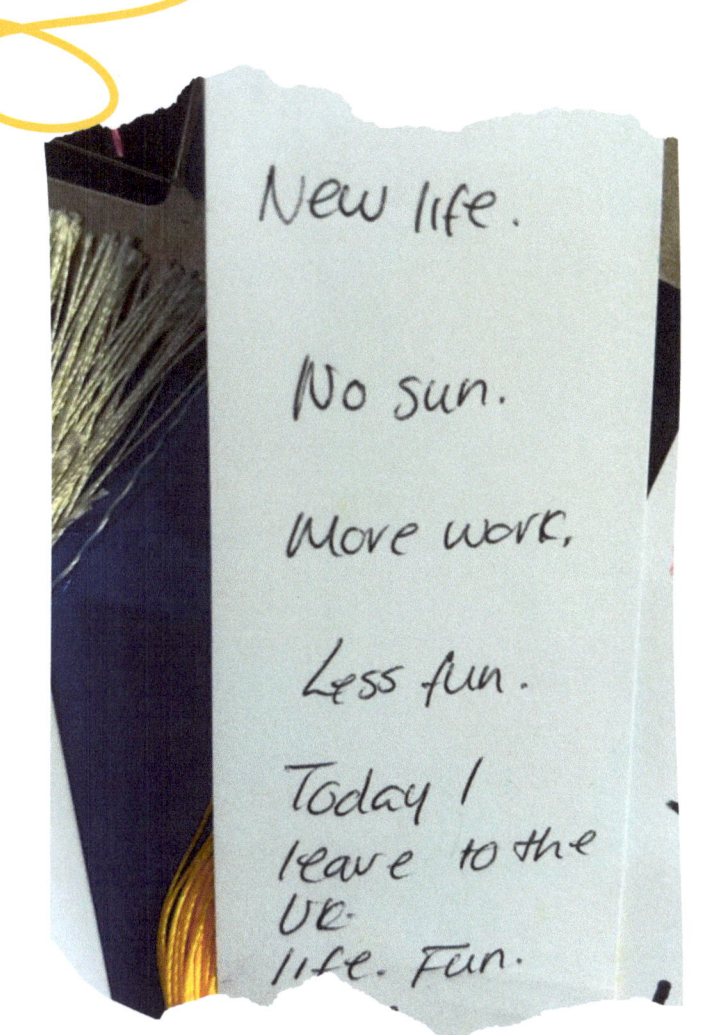

New life.

No sun.

More work.

Less fun.

Today I leave to the UK.
Life. Fun.

On a gigantic ship they came, with a special windrush name.

Leaving their homes a long long way, trying to find somewhere new to stay.

With excitement and bravery they set sail.
Facing challenges without fail.

UNDER THE MANGO TREE WORDSEARCH ONE

Find and circle the words.

M	T	F	A	M	I	L	Y	A	S	A	M	C
A	Y	A	E	R	J	O	U	R	N	E	Y	O
N	I	T	H	K	J	L	A	B	S	Y	R	M
G	S	H	W	O	N	S	D	T	W	E	N	M
O	K	E	F	S	M	E	A	T	S	R	I	U
R	E	R	D	T	L	E	U	H	H	U	C	N
P	G	R	E	E	R	Y	L	R	I	E	O	I
J	O	B	K	R	E	E	H	A	P	R	U	T
M	Y	M	I	Y	J	V	E	G	N	E	S	Y
A	U	N	M	O	T	H	E	R	T	D	I	E
K	I	S	L	A	N	D	R	K	Y	A	O	R
C	A	R	I	B	B	E	A	N	E	R	T	H

Mango   Tree   Homeland
Father   Job   Family
Journey   Mother   Community
Ship   Island   Caribbean

UNDER THE MANGO TREE WORDSEARCH TWO

Find and circle the words.

A	T	F	A	R	R	I	V	A	L	A	M	O
R	Y	A	E	R	H	O	P	E	N	C	I	P
R	I	T	H	K	J	G	A	S	S	O	G	P
I	S	H	W	I	N	S	R	E	W	C	R	O
V	K	E	F	E	S	E	A	A	S	O	A	R
A	E	R	M	T	L	T	U	H	H	N	T	T
L	G	O	E	E	R	Y	O	R	I	U	I	U
J	H	B	E	R	E	E	H	R	P	T	O	N
M	Y	L	I	L	J	V	E	G	Y	E	N	I
T	N	A	L	P	K	E	E	E	R	D	I	T
C	U	L	T	U	R	E	R	K	Y	A	O	Y
C	A	R	I	B	E	G	A	T	I	R	E	H

Plant   Home   Migration
Arrival   Sea   History
Coconut   Culture   Opportunity
Hope   Arrival   Heritage

ANSWERS ON THE NEXT PAGE

SEE HOW YOU DID!

Answers
UNDER THE MANGO TREE WORDSEARCH ONE

Find and circle the words.

M	T	F	A	M	I	L	Y	A	S	A	M	C
A	Y	A	E	R	J	O	U	R	N	E	Y	O
N	I	T	H	K	J	L	A	B	S	Y	R	M
G	S	H	W	O	N	S	D	T	W	E	N	M
O	K	E	F	S	M	E	A	T	S	R	I	U
R	E	R	D	T	L	E	U	H	H	U	C	N
P	G	R	E	E	R	Y	L	R	I	E	O	I
J	O	B	K	R	E	E	H	A	P	R	U	T
M	Y	M	I	Y	J	V	E	G	N	E	S	Y
A	U	N	M	O	T	H	E	R	T	D	I	E
K	I	S	L	A	N	D	R	K	Y	A	O	R
C	A	R	I	B	B	E	A	N	E	R	T	H

Mango   Tree   Homeland
Father   Job   Family
Journey   Mother   Community
Ship   Island   Caribbean

Answers
UNDER THE MANGO TREE WORDSEARCH TWO

Find and circle the words.

A	T	F	A	R	R	I	V	A	L	A	M	O
R	Y	A	E	R	H	O	P	E	N	C	I	P
R	I	T	H	K	J	G	A	S	S	O	G	P
I	S	H	W	I	N	S	R	E	W	C	R	O
V	K	E	F	E	S	E	A	A	S	O	A	R
A	E	R	M	T	L	T	U	H	H	N	T	T
L	G	O	E	E	R	Y	O	R	I	U	I	U
J	H	B	E	R	E	E	H	R	P	T	O	N
M	Y	L	I	L	J	V	E	G	Y	E	N	I
T	N	A	L	P	K	E	E	E	R	D	I	T
C	U	L	T	U	R	E	R	K	Y	A	O	Y
C	A	R	I	B	E	G	A	T	I	R	E	H

Plant   Home   Migration
Arrival   Sea   History
Coconut   Culture   Opportunity
Hope   Arrival   Heritage

Now it's your turn......

My Windrush Poem

My Windrush Poem

My Windrush Poem

My Windrush Poem

My Windrush Poem

My Windrush Poem

My Windrush Poem

My Windrush Poem

Partnerships:

LOGOS
Ideas that create brighter futures

www.ingramcontent.com/pod-product-compliance
Lightning Source LLC
Chambersburg PA
CBHW042247100526
44587CB00002B/50